BIGGEST NAMES IN SPORTS

DEREK CARR

FOOTBALL STAR

by Matt Scheff

FOCUS READERS

FOCUS READERS

WWW.FOCUSREADERS.COM

Focus Readers is distributed by North Star Editions:
sales@northstareditions.com | 888-417-0195

Produced for Focus Readers by Red Line Editorial.

Photographs ©: Mike Roemer/AP Images, cover, 1; Tom DiPace/AP Images, 4–5, 7; Jason Behnken/AP Images, 9; Eddy Matchette/Houston Chronicle/AP Images, 10–11; Thurman James/Cal Sports Media/AP Images, 13; John Green/Cal Sports Media/AP Images, 15; Marcio Jose Sanchez/AP Images, 16–17; Rex Features/AP Images, 19; Tony Avelar/AP Images, 21, 27; Bill Feig/AP Images, 22–23; Butch Dill/AP Images, 24; Red Line Editorial, 29

ISBN
978-1-63517-485-4 (hardcover)
978-1-63517-557-8 (paperback)
978-1-63517-701-5 (ebook pdf)
978-1-63517-629-2 (hosted ebook)

Library of Congress Control Number: 2017948063

Printed in the United States of America
Mankato, MN
November, 2017

ABOUT THE AUTHOR

Matt Scheff is an artist and author living in Alaska. He enjoys mountain climbing, deep-sea fishing, and curling up with his two Siberian huskies to watch football.

TABLE OF CONTENTS

CHAPTER 1

RECORD DAY

Derek Carr knew his team needed him. The Oakland Raiders were on the road facing the Tampa Bay Buccaneers late in the 2016 season. With four minutes left in the game, the Raiders trailed 24–17. Bucs fans roared. The hometown team just needed to keep the Raiders out of the end zone. But Carr had other ideas.

Carr had one of the best games of his career against the Bucs in 2016.

Carr and the Raiders started the drive at their own 25-yard line. Running a **no-huddle offense**, Carr kept Tampa's defense off balance. He zipped passes all over the field. The Raiders marched toward the goal line as the clock ticked away.

With 1:38 left in the game, Carr took a snap from Tampa's 7-yard line. He dropped back. The Tampa pass rush crashed in on him. Carr spotted tight end Mychal Rivera in the middle of the field. Carr didn't hesitate. He threw the ball to Rivera, threading it through tight **coverage**. Rivera hauled it in and fell into the end zone. The game was tied 24–24!

Carr attempts a pass from deep in his own end zone.

With the teams still tied, the game went into overtime. Neither team backed down. Oakland had the ball at Tampa's 41-yard line with less than two minutes to play. It was fourth down. The Raiders needed at least four yards. If they didn't get it, the Bucs would have the last chance to score.

Carr wasn't interested in four yards. He wanted more. Wide receiver Seth Roberts streaked across the middle of the field. Carr completed a strike to Roberts, who slipped past a defender. Roberts sprinted to the end zone for a touchdown. Carr raised his arms toward the sky. The Raiders stormed the field to celebrate a big victory.

Roberts and Carr celebrate after connecting on an overtime touchdown.

Carr's performance stands out in Raiders history. He finished the game with 513 passing yards. That was the most in the history of the team.

CLEMENTS
5

CHAPTER 2

FOOTBALL FAMILY

Derek Carr was born on March 28, 1991, in Fresno, California. He spent his early life in Bakersfield, California. Derek always loved sports, just like his older brothers David and Darren.

Derek was 12 years younger than his oldest brother, David. As Derek grew up, he spent lots of time watching David play.

Derek takes a breather during a 2006 high school game.

David was the star of his high school team. He later became one of the nation's top college quarterbacks at Fresno State. Derek was only 11 years old when the Houston Texans **drafted** David in 2002. The Carr family moved to Sugar Land, Texas, to be close to him.

TOUGH LOVE

When Derek was 10 years old, his brothers came to one of his youth football games. Derek took a hard hit. He marched to the bench and told the coach he was done playing for the day. His brothers didn't like that. They yelled at him to get back out on the field. Quitting was not an option, they explained. It was a lesson that stayed with Derek as he rose through the football ranks.

Carr shouts directions to his teammates before taking the snap.

David struggled in the National Football League (NFL). The Texans released him in 2007. Meanwhile, Derek was on a mission to blaze his own path.

He became the starting quarterback for Clements High School as a sophomore. For his senior year, Derek moved back to Bakersfield. He led his team to a state championship.

Just like his brother, Derek chose to attend Fresno State. In 2011, he took over as the school's starting quarterback. He threw 26 touchdown passes and only 9 **interceptions** as a sophomore. And he just kept getting better. During his senior year in 2013, he was one of the nation's top college players. He threw 50 touchdown passes and 8 interceptions. Carr was also in the running for the Heisman Trophy. That

Carr attempts a pass in a 2013 game against the University of Southern California.

honor goes to college football's best player. Carr didn't win the award, but he definitely had the attention of NFL **scouts**.

CARR
RAIDERS
4

CHAPTER 3

NFL DREAMS

As the 2014 NFL Draft approached, pro teams showed interest in Carr. However, not everyone agreed on what kind of a **prospect** he was. Many scouts praised his strong arm and quick feet. However, others said he wasn't tall enough. Many scouts also thought his hands were too small.

Carr works out at a rookie training camp after being drafted by the Raiders.

Carr watched the first round of the draft unfold. Three quarterbacks were selected, but Carr was still waiting. Finally, the Raiders chose him in the second round, with the 36th overall pick in the draft.

NAME RECOGNITION

David Carr's lack of NFL success in the early 2000s affected how many fans viewed Derek leading up to the 2014 NFL Draft. It may have hurt Derek's chances with NFL teams, too. Houston was badly in need of a quarterback in 2014. But the Texans passed on Derek twice. Reports said the Texans wouldn't even consider picking him. Many people believed that was because of the team's experience with his brother David a decade earlier.

Carr threw two touchdown passes in his first game as an NFL quarterback.

Carr came out strong in the 2014 preseason and earned the starting job. In the opening game of the 2014 season, Carr threw his first career touchdown pass. It was a 12-yard connection to wide receiver Rod Streater.

But Carr's **rookie** year was tough at times. The Raiders were not a good team. Even so, Carr started all 16 games and showed some flashes of his ability. The highlight came when he led the Raiders to a comeback win over the Kansas City Chiefs. Despite the victory, Raiders fans didn't have much to cheer for. The team finished the season with a 3–13 record.

Things started to turn around for Carr and the Raiders in 2015. In the second game of the season, Carr threw the winning touchdown pass against the Baltimore Ravens with just 26 seconds left in the game. Carr went on to throw 32 touchdown passes on the season. He

Carr pumps his fist after tossing a touchdown pass against the Ravens.

was even named to the Pro Bowl. The Raiders improved to 7–9 that year. They didn't make the playoffs, but they were improving.

CHAPTER 4

SUPERSTAR

The Raiders entered the 2016 season with high hopes. Carr wasted no time showing that he was one of the NFL's best passers. In the first game of the year, the Raiders trailed the New Orleans Saints 34–27. With just 47 seconds left in the game, Carr zipped a touchdown pass to wide receiver Seth Roberts.

Carr avoids the pass rush in a 2016 game against the Saints.

Carr flashes a big smile after pulling off an overtime win.

The Raiders could have tried for an extra point to tie the game. Instead, they went for a two-point conversion. The game came down to one play. Carr took the snap from the **shotgun**. He stepped back and then launched a high pass to the left corner of the end zone. Wide receiver Michael Crabtree stretched and hauled it in. The Raiders won the game 35–34.

That game set the tone for the Raiders' season. Carr led a powerful offense. And he was at his best when the game was on the line. Carr led the Raiders to seven fourth-quarter comebacks.

In Week 16, the Raiders faced the Indianapolis Colts. In the fourth quarter, the Colts defense sacked Carr. Carr remained on the ground after the play ended. He knew right away what had happened. His leg was broken.

Doctors told Carr that he would need six to eight weeks to recover. His season was over. The Raiders weren't the same team without him, and they lost their opening playoff game to the Texans.

Raiders fans were disappointed. But the season also gave them reason for hope.

GIVING BACK

Giving back to the community is important to Carr. One of his passions is helping children's hospitals. His son Dallas was born with serious health problems and spent weeks in the hospital. Doctors helped Dallas leave healthy. Now Derek works to help raise money for children's hospitals and also visits sick children.

Despite a tough end to the 2016 season, Carr had a spectacular year.

With Carr as their quarterback, Raiders fans were confident that the team would return to the playoffs. And Carr had extra motivation. In 2017, he signed a new contract with the Raiders. The deal made Carr the highest-paid player in the NFL.

DEREK CARR

- Height: 6 feet 3 inches (191 cm)
- Weight: 215 pounds (98 kg)
- Birth date: March 28, 1991
- Birthplace: Fresno, California
- High school: Clements High School (Sugar Land, Texas); Bakersfield Christian High School (Bakersfield, California)
- College: Fresno State (2009–2013)
- NFL team: Oakland Raiders (2014–)
- Major awards: Mountain West Player of the Year (2012, 2013); Pro Bowl (2015, 2016)

Oakland
Fresno
Bakersfield
Sugar Land

FOCUS ON

DEREK CARR

Write your answers on a separate piece of paper.

1. Write a sentence describing the main ideas of Chapter 3.
2. Do you think it was fair for teams to judge Derek based on his brother's NFL experience? Why or why not?
3. Why did the Carr family move to Texas?
    - **A.** so Derek could play for a better high school team
    - **B.** to be closer to David as he started his NFL career
    - **C.** because Derek's father got a new job
4. How did Carr's 2016 injury affect the Raiders?
    - **A.** It slowed down their offense.
    - **B.** It caused the team's offense to improve.
    - **C.** It had little effect on the team.

Answer key on page 32.

GLOSSARY

coverage

The way a football team defends an opponent's receivers.

drafted

Selected a player in a draft. A draft is a system that allows teams to acquire new players who are coming into a league.

interceptions

Plays in which the defense catches a pass, gaining possession of the ball.

no-huddle offense

An offense in which the quarterback calls plays at the line of scrimmage rather than in a huddle.

prospect

A player who is likely to be successful in the future.

rookie

A professional athlete in his or her first year.

scouts

People whose jobs involve looking for talented young players.

shotgun

A formation in which the quarterback starts several yards behind the line of scrimmage.

TO LEARN MORE

BOOKS

Kelley, Patrick. *Oakland Raiders*. Minneapolis: Abdo Publishing, 2016.

Morey, Allan. *The Oakland Raiders Story*. Minneapolis: Bellwether Media, 2017.

Silverman, Drew. *Today's NFL: 12 Reasons Fans Follow the Game*. North Mankato, MN: 12-Story Library, 2016.

NOTE TO EDUCATORS

Visit **www.focusreaders.com** to find lesson plans, activities, links, and other resources related to this title.

INDEX

Answer Key: 1. Answers will vary; **2.** Answers will vary; **3.** B; **4.** A